DELAWARE

Explore the United States

Sarah Tieck

Big Buddy BOOKS
Explore the United States

VISIT US AT

www.abdopublishing.com

Published by ABDO Publishing Company, PO Box 398166, Minneapolis, MN 55439.

Printed in the United States of America, North Mankato, Minnesota.
022012
092012

 PRINTED ON RECYCLED PAPER

Coordinating Series Editor: Rochelle Baltzer
Contributing Editors: Megan M. Gunderson, BreAnn Rumsch, Marcia Zappa
Graphic Design: Adam Craven
Cover Photograph: *iStockphoto*: ©iStockphoto.com/mdgmorris.
Interior Photographs/Illustrations: *Alamy*: Everett Collection Inc (p. 25), Edwin Remsberg (p. 30); *AP Photo*: North Wind Picture Archives via AP Images (pp. 13, 23), Nick Wass (p. 26); *Getty Images*: Dan Callister (p. 25), Jerry Markland/Getty Images for NASCAR (p. 21), Panoramic (p. 11), James Zipp/Photo Researchers (p. 30); *Glow Images*: Superstock (p. 9), Visions of America RM (p. 13); *iStockphoto*: ©iStockphoto.com/aimintang (pp. 9, 26), ©iStockphoto.com/Dobresum (p. 27), ©iStockphoto.com/Elisarose (p. 29), ©iStockphoto.com/ Jasmina007 (p. 27), ©iStockphoto.com/mdgmorris (p. 27), ©iStockphoto.com/Nnehring (p. 30), ©iStockphoto. com/WilliamSherman (p. 5); *Photo Researchers, Inc.*: Michael P. Gadomski (p. 17); *Shutterstock*: 4736202690 (p. 19), Phillip Lange (p. 30), rsooll (p. 23), Sveta San (p. 19).

All population figures taken from the 2010 US census.

Library of Congress Cataloging-in-Publication Data

Tieck, Sarah, 1976-
 Delaware / Sarah Tieck.
    p. cm. -- (Explore the United States)
 ISBN 978-1-61783-346-5
 1. Delaware--Juvenile literature. I. Title.
 F164.3.T49 2013
 975.1--dc23
                        2012000830

DELAWARE

Contents

One Nation 4

Delaware Up Close 6

Important Cities 8

Delaware in History 12

Timeline 14

Across the Land 16

Earning a Living 18

Sports Page 20

Hometown Heroes 22

Tour Book 26

A Great State 28

Fast Facts 30

Important Words 31

Web Sites 31

Index 32

ONE NATION

The United States is a **diverse** country. It has farmland, cities, coasts, and mountains. Its people come from many different backgrounds. And, its history covers more than 200 years.

Today the country includes 50 states. Delaware is one of these states. Let's learn more about Delaware and its story!

Did You Know?

Delaware became a state on December 7, 1787. It was the first state in the nation!

4

DELAWARE UP CLOSE

The United States has four main **regions**. Delaware is in the South.

Delaware has three states on its borders. Pennsylvania is north. Maryland is west and south. And New Jersey is east. Delaware Bay and the Atlantic Ocean are also east.

Delaware is the second-smallest state. It has a total area of just 2,023 square miles (5,240 sq km). About 900,000 people live there.

REGIONS OF THE UNITED STATES

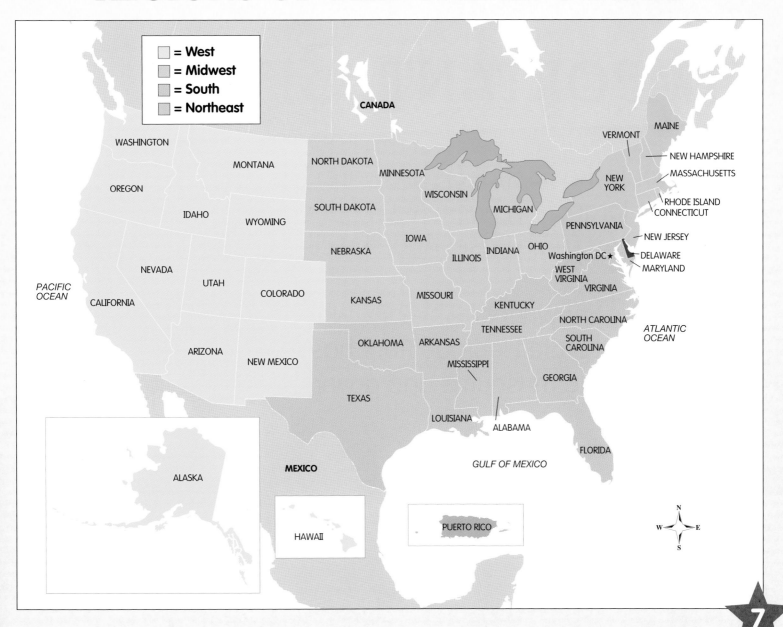

Legend:
- ☐ = West
- ☐ = Midwest
- ☐ = South
- ☐ = Northeast

CANADA

WASHINGTON
MONTANA
NORTH DAKOTA
MINNESOTA
VERMONT
MAINE
NEW HAMPSHIRE
OREGON
IDAHO
WYOMING
SOUTH DAKOTA
WISCONSIN
MICHIGAN
NEW YORK
MASSACHUSETTS
RHODE ISLAND
CONNECTICUT
NEVADA
UTAH
COLORADO
NEBRASKA
IOWA
ILLINOIS
INDIANA
OHIO
PENNSYLVANIA
NEW JERSEY
DELAWARE
MARYLAND
Washington DC ★
WEST VIRGINIA
VIRGINIA
CALIFORNIA
KANSAS
MISSOURI
KENTUCKY
PACIFIC OCEAN
ARIZONA
NEW MEXICO
OKLAHOMA
ARKANSAS
TENNESSEE
NORTH CAROLINA
SOUTH CAROLINA
ATLANTIC OCEAN
MISSISSIPPI
GEORGIA
TEXAS
LOUISIANA
ALABAMA
FLORIDA
GULF OF MEXICO
MEXICO
ALASKA
HAWAII
PUERTO RICO

N
W E
S

Important Cities

Dover is the **capital** of Delaware. It is also the state's second-largest city, with 36,047 people. Dover is home to Dover Air Force Base. And, the city is surrounded by farmland.

Dover is known for its history, which dates to 1683. Today, First State Heritage Park has several historic sites. These include museums and government buildings.

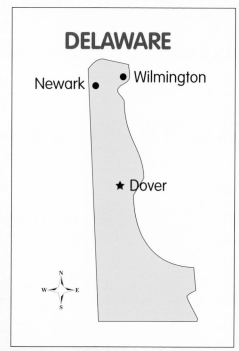

DELAWARE

Newark ● ● Wilmington

★ Dover

Old State House (*above*) and Legislative Hall (*right*) are part of First State Heritage Park.

Wilmington is Delaware's largest city. It is home to 70,851 people. The DuPont Company started near there in 1802. It helped the city grow. Today, the company makes products from paint to seeds.

Newark is the state's third-largest city, with 31,454 people. The University of Delaware began there in 1743. It is known for its work in science.

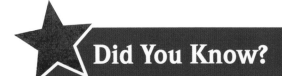

Did You Know?

Wilmington became a railroad hub around 1838. Today, it has a busy Amtrak train station.

Wilmington is on the Delaware River. Ships use its port to drop off and pick up goods.

11

DELAWARE IN HISTORY

Delaware's history includes early settlers and the beginning of the United States. In 1609, explorer Henry Hudson visited Delaware. Swedish settlers came to the area in 1638. Later, England ruled the settlements.

By 1775, colonists no longer wanted to be ruled by England. So that year, they began fighting in the **Revolutionary War**. They won in 1783. In 1787, Delaware became the first state in the nation.

In 1609, Hudson sailed from Holland to North America on the *Half Moon*.

★ **Did You Know?**

Delaware was named for Lord De La Warr. In 1610, he arrived in nearby Jamestown Colony. He brought supplies to save the settlers from dying.

In the 1600s, Swedish settlers built North America's first log cabins in Delaware.

Timeline

1704

New Castle became the **capital** of Delaware, which was ruled by England.

1775

Colonists began fighting in the **Revolutionary War**.

1776

Thomas McKean, George Read, and Caesar Rodney of Delaware signed the **Declaration of Independence**.

1777

Dover became the new capital of Delaware.

1787

Delaware became the first state on December 7.

1838

A railroad was built that connected Wilmington with Baltimore and Philadelphia. This helped businesses grow.

1700s

1800s

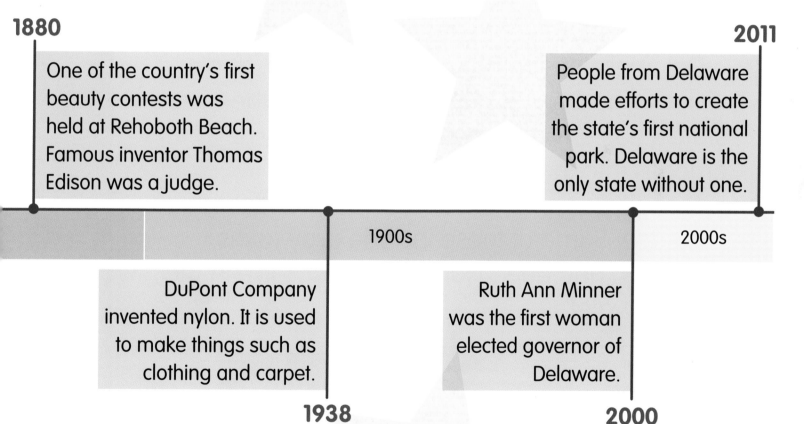

1880

One of the country's first beauty contests was held at Rehoboth Beach. Famous inventor Thomas Edison was a judge.

2011

People from Delaware made efforts to create the state's first national park. Delaware is the only state without one.

1900s

2000s

DuPont Company invented nylon. It is used to make things such as clothing and carpet.

Ruth Ann Minner was the first woman elected governor of Delaware.

1938

2000

15

Across the Land

Delaware has beaches, harbors, hills, and valleys. The Delaware River runs down the state's eastern border. At Delaware Bay, it empties into the Atlantic Ocean.

Many types of animals make their homes in this state. Some of these include gray foxes, raccoons, and deer. Horseshoe crabs live in the coastal waters.

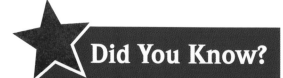

Did You Know?

Delaware has mild weather. Its average July high temperature is about 86°F (30°C). In January, its average low is about 23°F (-5°C).

Trap Pond State Park became one of Delaware's first
state parks in 1951. It has a swamp thick with trees.

17

Earning a Living

Delaware is a state rich with **resources** and businesses. Finance, **insurance**, and **real estate** companies all provide jobs. **Chemicals**, food products, rubber, and plastics are made in Delaware. Sand and gravel are mined there. And, the state's farms provide soybeans, corn, and milk.

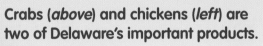

Crabs (*above*) and chickens (*left*) are two of Delaware's important products.

Sports Page

Many people think of car races when they think of Delaware. That's because the state is home to the Dover International Speedway. Two important NASCAR races are held there each year!

NASCAR stands for the National Association for Stock Car Auto Racing. These popular races are held around the country.

Hometown Heroes

Many famous people have lived in Delaware. Caesar Rodney was born in Dover in 1728. He is famous for helping fight for freedom from England. In 1776, he was one of the men who signed the **Declaration of Independence**.

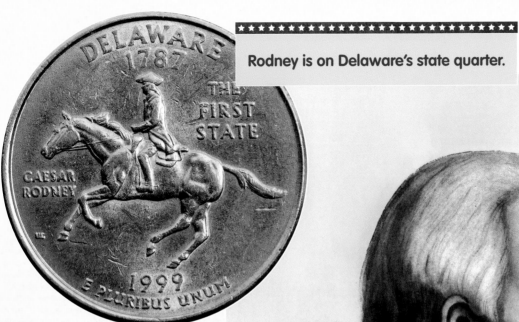

Rodney is on Delaware's state quarter.

★★

Rodney raced on horseback to vote for independence from England.

23

E.I. du Pont was born in France in 1771. He moved to America in 1800. In 1802, he founded the DuPont Company near Wilmington. This company grew large. It helped Delaware become a strong state.

Henry Heimlich was born in Wilmington in 1920. In 1974, he shared a way to stop people from choking. This method was called the Heimlich maneuver. It is still used today!

Thomas Jefferson told E.I. du Pont (*above*) to start a business making gunpowder. Jefferson wanted the new company to supply the United States.

Heimlich taught others how to stop people from choking.

25

Tour Book

Do you want to go to Delaware? If you visit the state, here are some places to go and things to do!

 ## See

Delaware Bay has more horseshoe crabs than anywhere else in the world! These crabs are useful creatures. Scientists study their eyes to learn more about human eyes. And, part of their shell is used to make bandages.

 ## Cheer

Take in a NASCAR race at the Dover International Speedway.

 ## Taste

Eat some Delaware strawberries, which are known for their flavor. Seafood is also popular, since Delaware is on the Atlantic coast.

 ## Discover

Winterthur Museum in Wilmington is known for its library and gardens.

 ## Explore

Spend a day at Rehoboth Beach. Build a sand castle or look for seashells on this famous beach!

A GREAT STATE

The story of Delaware is important to the United States. The people and places that make up this state offer something special to the country. Together with all the states, Delaware helps make the United States great.

Delaware's coast is known for its beautiful beaches.

Fast Facts

Date of Statehood:
December 7, 1787

Population (rank):
897,934
(45th most-populated state)

Total Area (rank):
2,023 square miles
(49th largest state)

Motto:
"Liberty and Independence"

Nickname:
First State,
Diamond State

State Capital:
Dover

Flag:

Flower: Peach Blossom

Postal Abbreviation:
DE

Tree: American Holly

Bird: Blue Hen Chicken

Important Words

capital a city where government leaders meet.

chemical (KEH-mih-kuhl) a substance that can cause reactions and changes.

Declaration of Independence a very important paper in American history. It announces the separation of the American colonies from Great Britain.

diverse made up of things that are different from each other.

insurance a contract that promises to guard people against a loss of money if something happens to them or their property.

real estate the business of selling buildings and land.

region a large part of a country that is different from other parts.

resource a supply of something useful or valued.

Revolutionary War a war fought between England and the North American colonies from 1775 to 1783.

Web Sites

To learn more about Delaware, visit ABDO Publishing Company online. Web sites about Delaware are featured on our Book Links page. These links are routinely monitored and updated to provide the most current information available.

www.abdopublishing.com

Index

American colonies **12, 13, 14**
animals **16, 26, 30**
Atlantic Ocean **6, 16, 27**
businesses **10, 14, 15, 18, 19, 24, 25**
De La Warr, Lord **13**
Declaration of Independence **14, 22**
Delaware Bay **5, 6, 16, 26**
Delaware River **11, 16**
Dover **8, 14, 20, 22, 26, 30**
Dover Air Force Base **8**
du Pont, E.I. **24, 25**
DuPont Company **10, 15, 24**
Edison, Thomas **15**
England **12, 14, 22, 23**
First State Heritage Park **8, 9**
France **24**
Heimlich, Henry **24, 25**
Holland **13**
Hudson, Henry **12, 13**

Jefferson, Thomas **25**
McKean, Thomas **14**
Minner, Ruth Ann **15**
New Castle **14**
Newark **10**
population **6, 8, 10, 30**
Read, George **14**
Rehoboth Beach **15, 27**
Revolutionary War **12, 14**
Rodney, Caesar **14, 22, 23**
size **6, 30**
South (region) **6**
statehood **4, 12, 14, 30**
Sweden **12, 13**
Trap Pond State Park **17**
University of Delaware **10**
weather **16**
Wilmington **10, 11, 14, 24, 27**
Winterthur Museum **27**